FORENSIC PSYCHOLOGY WORKBOOK

CONNOR WHITELEY

Copyright © 2020 CONNOR WHITELEY

All rights reserved.

DEDICATION

Thank you to all my readers who continue to support me
and my work without you I couldn't do what I love.

INTRODUCTION TO FORENSIC PSYCHOLOGY

What is forensic psychology?

....
....
....
....
....
....
....

What areas of psychology are related to forensic psychology?

....
....
....
....
....
....
....
....
....
....

What areas of psychology can you work?

How does forensic psychology help the progression of justice?

....
....
....
....
....

What attitudes and philosophical perspectives should you have in forensic psychology?

....
....
....
....
....
....
....
....
....
....
....
....
....

What's the history of forensic psychology?

....
....
....
....
....
....

Connor Whiteley

How has forensic psychology developed an infrastructure to maintain its continued existence?

THEORIES OF OFFENDING
What categories can offending theories be put in?

How does social learning theory help to explain offending?

Name some examples of reinforcers.

Critically evaluate social learning theory.

Explain the cognitive theory of crime.

Explain how self-regulation and risk behaviour can cause people to offend.

Explain the biosocial theory of crime.

What factors can cause children to offend?

Explain how video games cause violence.

What's the problem with this idea?

Explain and evaluate the sociocultural theory.

Explain and evaluate Organisation theory

Explain and evaluate Sex role spillover theory

Explain and evaluate Biological theory

Explain and evaluate Four-factor theory

Explain neuropsychological as a theory of offending

Explain and evaluate addiction

What are the 5 types of rapists ad who proposed the types?

PUBLIC AND CRIME

What are the stages of crime according to Ainsworth (2000)?

Why is the fear of crime important in a political context?

What is the fear-victimisation paradox and who created it?

Is the fear of crime a phobia?

Explain cultivation theory

....
....
....
....

Explain Availability heuristic theory

....
....
....
....
....
....
....
....
....
....
....
....

Explain Cognitive theory

....
....
....
....
....
....
....
....
....

What's restorative justice and its outcome?

What factors can impact a victim's decision to report a crime?

What is secondary victimisation and how can it occur?

What's vicarious victimisation and how can therapists be victimised according to Campbell (1994)

....

Explain the stress-response theory of PTSD by Horowrite (1986)

....

What did the Halliday report (Home Office, 2000) say about public opinion and crime?

What are the political consequences of ignoring the public?

Why is the police-public relationship reciprocal?

Explain why listening to the public is justified?

IMPRISONMENT, PUISHMENT AND TREATMENT

Explain the humanitarian approach.

Explain the utilitarian approach.

Explain the retribution approach.

Explain depression theory

Explain Importation theory

Explain the point of imprisonment in the 16th century.

Explain the point of imprisonment in the 18th century

What did John Howard insist on?

Explain the point of imprisonment in the 19th century

Explain the point of imprisonment in the 20th century

Based on research, does capital punishment detect offending?

Name two ineffective approaches to research.

Discuss cognitive and behavioural treatment and why is it effective for treatment.

Why do we treat offenders?

Define rehabilitation.

Explain the Good Lives Model.

Define primary goods

Give examples of primary goods.

Explain how group sex offender treatment works.

Explain what happens in each session of the National Anger Management Package.

Explain the 3 principles of the Risk-Need-Response Model.

FORENSIC PSYCHOLOGY WORKBOOK

COURTS
What 3 offences are heard at the Magistrates Court?

What 3 offences are heard at the Crown Court?

Explain how the Youth Justice System works and compare it to the adult Justice System.

FORENSIC PSYCHOLOGY WORKBOOK

Explain what the Adversarial System is.

Explain the Inquisitorial System.

Explain what the Procurator Fiscals are.

Define the terms Mens Rea and Actus Reus.

https://www.subscribepage.com/psychologyboxset

Thank you for reading.

I hoped you enjoyed it.

If you want a FREE book and keep up to date about new books and project. Then please sign up for my newsletter at www.connorwhiteley.net/

Have a great day.

CHECK OUT THE PSYCHOLOGY WORLD PODCAST FOR MORE PSYCHOLOGY INFORMATION!

AVAILABLE ON ALL MAJOR PODCAST APPS.

About the author:

Connor Whiteley is the author of over 30 books in the sci-fi fantasy, nonfiction psychology and books for writer's genre and he is a Human Branding Speaker and Consultant.

He is a passionate warhammer 40,000 reader, psychology student and author.

Who narrates his own audiobooks and he hosts The Psychology World Podcast.

All whilst studying Psychology at the University of Kent, England.

Also, he was a former Explorer Scout where he gave a speech to the Maltese President in August 2018 and he attended Prince Charles' 70th Birthday Party at Buckingham Palace in May 2018.

Plus, he is a self-confessed coffee lover!

Please follow me on:

Website: www.connorwhiteley.net

Twitter: @scifiwhiteley

Please leave on honest review as this helps with the discoverability of the book and I truly appreciate it.

Thank you for reading. I hope you've enjoyed.

All books in 'An Introductory Series':

BIOLOGICAL PSYCHOLOGY 3RD EDITION

COGNITIVE PSYCHOLOGY 2ND EDITION

SOCIAL PSYCHOLOGY- 3RD EDITION

ABNORMAL PSYCHOLOGY 3RD EDITION

PSYCHOLOGY OF RELATIONSHIPS- 3RD EDITION

DEVELOPMENTAL PSYCHOLOGY 3RD EDITION

HEALTH PSYCHOLOGY

RESEARCH IN PSYCHOLOGY

A GUIDE TO MENTAL HEALTH AND TREATMENT AROUND THE WORLD- A GLOBAL LOOK AT DEPRESSION

FORENSIC PSYCHOLOGY

CLINICAL PSYCHOLOGY

FORMULATION IN PSYCHOTHERAPY

Other books by Connor Whiteley:

THE ANGEL OF RETURN

THE ANGEL OF FREEDOM

GARRO: GALAXY'S END

GARRO: RISE OF THE ORDER

GARRO: END TIMES

GARRO: SHORT STORIES

GARRO: COLLECTION

GARRO: HERESY

GARRO: FAITHLESS

GARRO: DESTROYER OF WORLDS

GARRO: COLLECTIONS BOOK 4-6

GARRO: MISTRESS OF BLOOD

GARRO: BEACON OF HOPE

GARRO: END OF DAYS

WINTER'S COMING

WINTER'S HUNT

WINTER'S REVENGE

WINTER'S DISSENSION

Companion guides:

BIOLOGICAL PSYCHOLOGY 2ND EDITION WORKBOOK

COGNITIVE PSYCHOLOGY 2ND EDITION WORKBOOK

SOCIOCULTURAL PSYCHOLOGY 2ND EDITION WORKBOOK

ABNORMAL PSYCHOLOGY 2ND EDITION WORKBOOK

PSYCHOLOGY OF HUMAN RELATIONSHIPS 2ND EDITION WORKBOOK

HEALTH PSYCHOLOGY WORKBOOK

FORENSIC PSYCHOLOGY WORKBOOK

Audiobooks by Connor Whiteley:

BIOLOGICAL PSYCHOLOGY

COGNITIVE PSYCHOLOGY

SOCIOCULTURAL PSYCHOLOGY

ABNORMAL PSYCHOLOGY

PSYCHOLOGY OF HUMAN RELATIONSHIPS

HEALTH PSYCHOLOGY

DEVELOPMENTAL PSYCHOLOGY

RESEARCH IN PSYCHOLOGY

FORENSIC PSYCHOLOGY

GARRO: GALAXY'S END

GARRO: RISE OF THE ORDER

GARRO: SHORT STORIES

GARRO: END TIMES

GARRO: COLLECTION

GARRO: HERESY

GARRO: FAITHLESS

GARRO: DESTROYER OF WORLDS

GARRO: COLLECTION BOOKS 4-6

GARRO: COLLECTION BOOKS 1-6

Business books:

TIME MANAGEMENT: A GUIDE FOR STUDENTS AND WORKERS

LEADERSHIP: WHAT MAKES A GOOD LEADER? A GUIDE FOR STUDENTS AND WORKERS.

BUSINESS SKILLS: HOW TO SURVIVE THE BUSINESS WORLD? A GUIDE FOR STUDENTS, EMPLOYEES AND EMPLOYERS.

BUSINESS COLLECTION

GET YOUR FREE BOOK AT:
WWW.CONNORWHITELEY.NET

www.ingramcontent.com/pod-product-compliance
Lightning Source LLC
LaVergne TN
LVHW012125070526
838202LV00056B/5864